Edward Lowell Anderson

Curb, Snaffle, and Spur

A Method of Training Young Horses for the Cavalry Service

Edward Lowell Anderson

Curb, Snaffle, and Spur
A Method of Training Young Horses for the Cavalry Service

ISBN/EAN: 9783744678230

Printed in Europe, USA, Canada, Australia, Japan

Cover: Foto ©Andreas Hilbeck / pixelio.de

More available books at **www.hansebooks.com**

THE GALLOP ABOUT A LANCE.

CURB, SNAFFLE, AND SPUR.

A METHOD OF TRAINING YOUNG HORSES
FOR THE CAVALRY SERVICE,

AND

FOR GENERAL USE UNDER THE SADDLE.

BY

EDWARD L. ANDERSON,

AUTHOR OF "MODERN HORSEMANSHIP."

Illustrated by Thirty-two Photographs from the Life.

BOSTON:

LITTLE, BROWN, AND COMPANY.

EDINBURGH: DAVID DOUGLAS.

1894.

PREFACE.

————•————

THIS little work has been written especially with a view of presenting a method of training horses for the use of mounted soldiers; but there is nothing herein recommended that would not be important, if not absolutely necessary, for the education of any horse intended for the saddle.

How long it would take to carry a horse through the course I have laid down would depend upon the age, strength, and disposition of each horse. The lessons might extend from the time the colt is weaned until it is four years old; or a strong three-year-old, with two short lessons daily, might be thoroughly trained in three months.

Five horses were brought before the camera for the illustration of the book. Silvana, now many years in service, was employed to explain the advanced exercises; Coquette, an English-bred mare, is represented in the frontispiece ; and three young horses which were photographed from the day the author took them in hand. These latter three had been broken to harness, and were quiet to handle, but had received no training such as they were then given, and they had all of the awkwardness and rigidity that could be desired.   I have found that a horse wholly undisciplined is of but little service before the camera when certain positions are required. The photographs were taken by Rombach and Groene, of Cincinnati, and the half-tone repro-ductions were made by the Heliotype Printing Company, of Boston.

CONTENTS.

Part I.

IN THE SNAFFLE.

Part II.

IN THE DOUBLE-REINED BRIDLE.

ILLUSTRATIONS.

Part I.

IN THE SNAFFLE.

CURB, SNAFFLE, AND SPUR.

CHAPTER I.

HANDLING THE YOUNG HORSE.

IT must be understood at the outset that in the
method of training presented in the following
pages the object of the work described is to
obtain immediate and exact control over the
horse, through a kindly enforced discipline, in
which nothing is left to the volition or willing
obedience of the animal. The muscular actions
which would impulsively follow the applications
of the hand and heel are to be cultivated in the
proper directions, so that the horse shall instinctively answer to the demands of its rider under all
circumstances. We are not to depend upon the
intelligence or the good-will of the animal, beyond
acquiring its confidence to such an extent that
its fears are not aroused by any movement the
trainer may make; and neither whip nor spur

should be used in punishment, — the correction
of faults, whether voluntary or involuntary, being
obtained by the control which will follow the true
use of the aids. The horse should not be taught
to regard any motions, words, or bugle-calls; for
it might obey such signals at inopportune times.
The silent application of the aids is the proper
manner for the rider to indicate his demands, and
the horse will be the readier to obey if it be
unused to preparatory signals. The trainer must
soothe by kind tones the young horse in its early
lessons, and he may correct it by a harsh voice;
but as soon as he acquires the confidence of the
animal, and it begins to understand the bit and
the spur, the man should conduct the lessons in
silence, and depend upon the aids for enforcing
his requirements. I know of nothing that seems
to give such pleasure and such satisfaction to
the horse as a slight relaxation upon the tension of the reins, and an almost imperceptible touch of the bridle-hand upon the crest,
when the rider wishes to encourage or reward
his mount. The horse very soon learns the
meaning of this, and how to appreciate it; and
as long as it does not affect the speed, direc-

tion, or carriage of the trained animal, I see nothing objectionable in it. This is the method followed by some of the best horsemen. One of these, a professional trainer, is so successful in his management of vicious horses, that I have frequently heard him say that he did not find anything wrong in certain animals which were turned over to his care as unruly by their owners.

The education of the horse cannot be begun too early. There is no reason why a yearling should not be as thoroughly disciplined as an old-school horse, and the early training will last during the life of the animal. Training does not injuriously affect the vivacity or the spirit of the horse; on the contrary, a cold-blooded drudge can be made active and mettlesome by a course of schooling. Witness Alidor, the horse employed to furnish the photographs for the first edition of " Modern Horsemanship," a coarse, heavy colt, which was brought to perform the high-school movements with grace and precision. The mare which was used for most of the illustrations in the present work, better bred than Alidor, is an example of the fact that a long

course of training is beneficial; for at fifteen
years she is full of life, mettle, and action, although a child might ride her. I wish to say
here that there is one class of horses that it is
useless to attempt to train or to use. These are
such that from deficiency in cranial development,
or from some lesion or injury to the brain, are
subject to fits of terror and wild excitement ; for
although even these may be taught to obey the
aids, their attacks are frequently so sudden that
the rider is in peril before he can attempt to
obtain control. The outward conformation sometimes marks these animals, even to the inexperi-
enced, and I have never known the small, pro-
tuberant eye (known as the buck's eye) fail to
give true warning that its possessor is a dangerous and useless fool.

With the young horse brought to the trainer
already disciplined from its early days, or with the
three-year-old simply halter-broken, we should
proceed in the same manner, although in the
first instance the preliminary lessons would be
far shorter, and rather as a test to see how far
the discipline had been carried. The cavesson
(a leather head-collar with a jointed metal nose-

band, having a ring at either side and one in
front) will be placed upon the horse, a strong
line, at least fifteen feet long, being attached to
the metal nose-band ring. The animal should
be led to some retired place, where there is
sufficient ground upon which to conduct the
exercises. A covered school is preferable for
the whole work of training, as the man can then
have the attention of the horse; but wherever
the work is carried on, there should be such
quiet as can be had. It is true that a school-
broken horse must be made acquainted with
many strange and new sights when it is first
taken out; but every young horse has to go
through such experiences, and it is much easier
to control the disciplined horse under these
circumstances than the raw colt, which has not
been taught to obey hand and heel. The man
should be perfectly composed, and he should
avoid doing anything that will arouse the fears
of the horse. He should lead the colt in a
circle of about thirty feet in diameter, first to
one hand and then to the other, walking at
its shoulder, and holding the line at about
eighteen inches from the nose-ring. If the

colt refuses to lead, as it probably will, the man must wait upon it. If he tries to force it to lead, the frightened animal will sulk, and all acknowledged resistances are to be avoided. It is likely that in a very short time it will become irksome to the colt to remain still, and at its first motion the trainer should let it move off, and encourage it as though the whole incident had been in accordance with his desires. The trainer should, from time to time, stop the colt, and then make it resume its round. The trainer's aim from this time forth should be, that the colt shall not volunteer a movement; or should it become necessary for him to take advantage of a voluntary movement after a refusal, the animal should be led to believe that it has really obeyed the man. During the circles, at the walk and at the halts, the man should handle the colt, as far as he can, without arousing its fears, — picking up its feet, patting it on various parts of its body, and rubbing the poll, never of course letting go of the line. The trainer will gradually lengthen his hold on the line, depending upon the behavior of the colt, until he has the animal walking about

him at its full length. He will bring the colt
to a halt by gently waving the line horizontally,
and he should then go quietly up to the animal
and make much of it. The colt must not be
allowed to come in to the man, but should, as
far as possible, be made to stop and stand in
the path of the circle. If the colt moves off
without permission, the man should bring it to
a halt, and then demand that it move, so that,
from the earliest lessons, it will learn to look
to the man for orders. These lessons will
interest and exercise the horse, and may be
conducted as long as the trainer sees fit, provided
he does not fatigue the animal. When the colt
will walk about the man quietly, and come to
a halt as he requires it, the trainer may put it
into a slow trot, using great care not to excite
the colt or to permit it to go too rapidly. He
should then teach it to come to a halt and
turn about for a change of direction. During
the longeing lessons the trainer should teach
the horse to bear the whip, which should never
be applied with any severity, a simple tap being
all that should be given, and this touch will
answer every requirement. The horse having

been taught to enjoy caresses, the rider should frequently pat and handle the animal while holding the short whip in his hand. Gradually he should habituate the horse to bear the whip

RUBBING THE COLT WITH THE WHIP.

as it is passed over various parts of the legs and body, and finally to move forward at a slight tap delivered upon the rump. The horse must not flinch at the motion or at the touch of the whip. A long whip should then be substituted for the riding-rod, and the trainer should use it with great discretion in stimulating the horse, by light touches given against the sides, or by striking the ground in rear of the animal, to increased speed and action on the longeing circles, it of course being understood that the rate of speed on the longeing circles should always be moderate. Should the horse be too eager or too much excited to obey the horizontal waves of the longe-line when the trainer wishes to reduce the speed or to demand a halt, a series of motions of the line up and down, with a strong pull on the line as it comes down, will have the greatest effect upon the cavesson; but this severe use of the longe-line is to be avoided. The exercises upon the longe will be continued until the horse is given sufficient work under the saddle; and during these, the trainer cannot use too much caution in securing the horse from fright or excitement.

CHAPTER II.

A CERTAIN amount of discipline having been established while upon the cavesson, and the young horse having found that there is nothing to dread in the approach or in the touch of its master, we arrive at the most important, and not the least difficult, part of the education of the animal. The manner in which the colt is taught to bear its rider will have a very marked influence upon its future usefulness; but any man of ordinary intelligence should be able to make the colt quiet to ride, if he be patient and firm. The horse should be saddled with care, the girths being but moderately tight, and the stirrups arranged so that they shall not touch the sides of the horse. The horse must now be taught something of the effects of the bit. I find that this, and some other matters connected with the general progress of the training, can be accomplished very readily by the trainer driving the horse before him for a few times, a pair of light long lines being run through the loops on the surcingle to an easy snaffle-bit. The horse should be driven in circles and upon straight lines, being frequently brought to a halt and then started forward, the trainer using as little force on the bit as is possible, and employing a long straight whip with caution. If at any time the animal kicks or rushes forward, it should be corrected by a sharp pull upon the reins. I have seen horses made confirmed kickers by the application of the whip as a corrective measure, and by the use of whip blows the horse may be taught to kick when it is even threatened. The horse that kicks must be corrected by having its head thrown up; and any horse can be taught to bear the whip, properly used, by gradual lessons, without flinching or resentment. During the halts in these lessons, the trainer should from time to time loosen and tighten the girths to accustom the horse to such handling, and he should occasionally bear some weight with his arms upon the saddle. The

trainer should induce the horse to submit to
be driven with the stirrups let out to the full
length of the leathers, and dangling against the
sides, and to bear the flapping of cloths over

ELEVATION OF HEAD.

any part of its body or legs. I may say here
that it is difficult to give these lessons when the
horse is annoyed by flies or other insects, as
the animal is apt to kick at the application of
whip or heel under such circumstances.

In mounting the colt for the first time the trainer should select an occasion when, after some gentle exercise, the animal is composed and confident. He should see that the snaffle-bridle is in good order, that it fits the head and mouth without discomfort, and that the saddle is properly and strongly girthed. If he has reason to believe that the horse will make violent resistances, he can insure his seat by having a rolled blanket strapped to the pommel of the saddle; but it is an exceptional horse that will give trouble, if its education has been conducted on the lines recommended. In riding a young or difficult horse for the first time, I prefer to have a leg up from an assistant; for in that way the rider can quietly obtain his seat before the animal can prevent, and this is a moral victory which the colt will understand. Should the trainer elect to mount in the usual way, he must take care that he does not irritate the horse by a thrust of the left toe, and that he does not strike the rump as he carries the right leg over. Once in the saddle, he should let the colt walk off as quietly as it will, the reins just taking a bearing upon the animal's mouth, and his heels away from its flanks. In this first

lesson the man should do very little beyond
letting the colt go quietly forward in a walk.
Unless something frightens the animal, it is not
probable that it will show any misconduct. If,
after a few minutes, all goes well, the rider should
quietly dismount, and resume the exercises upon
the longe-line. Upon the second time of mounting, the same precaution should be taken ; and on
each succeeding day the time during which the
man is on the colt's back may be gradually
extended, depending upon its strength and conduct. Perhaps on the fourth or fifth time that it
is mounted, the novelty of the situation having
worn off, the colt may take notice of surrounding
things, and if an excuse may be found in a bark-
ing dog, a flying bird, or some such matter, it
may pretend to be frightened, and give a few
plunges. If the rider will gently keep up its head,
and let it go forward in any slow pace or action
it will take, the colt will be convinced that it has
gained nothing by its efforts, and will not be
likely to repeat its misconduct except under some
provocation. Gradually the trainer will take
more command over the movements of the horse,
turning it to the right or the left, bringing it to a

halt and resuming the forward movement, putting it into a trot and bringing it back to a walk, accustoming it to the pressure of the legs against the flanks and even to light whip-taps behind the

BENDING HEAD.

girths to incite it to action. The hand should be ready but light, and the colt's head should be held well up. Plunging and bucking are the only disorders which are not due to the trainer's mismanagement, and these are the natural de-

fences of the horse. The former is a coltish
prank, which may become a fixed vice by bad
handling ; the latter is seldom found in horses of
domestic breeds, and is perhaps due as much to
tight girthing and rough " breaking " as to the
instinctive resistances of the half-wild animals in
which the vice is commonly found.

The precautions which I have so strongly in-
sisted upon may seem to some readers to be greater
than the matter requires ; but if the best results are
to be obtained, a trainer cannot observe too much
care in the treatment of the colt in these early
lessons. The critical period of the colt's education having been passed, and the animal having
been brought to carry its rider quietly, we must
extend the discipline, which up to this time has
been as little irksome as possible.

A most important thing is to teach the horse
to go into the bridle. Nearly every vice and
resistance offered by a horse is preceded and
made possible by the animal getting behind the
hand ; that is, it refuses to face the bit, so that the
rider's hand can find nothing by which he can
enforce his demands. The horse is taught to go
into the bridle by gently pushing it forward in a

slow trot against a light but constant tension of the reins. In time, by proceedings which we shall afterwards describe, the mouth of the horse may be made so elastic and light that it will answer to the gentlest drawing of the rein, always giving something upon which to act, but without rigidity or opposition. At first I do not hesitate to give my young horses mouths rather too hard than too soft, and I make them hold the head rather higher than is necessary for the union and balance of the extremities. This confirms them in facing the bit, and insures against the usual habit of too low a carriage of the head. Any condition of the mouth may be given the horse : a hard hand makes a hard mouth, a light hand a light mouth, and a nerveless hand lets the horse get behind the bit, and gives no mouth. During these lessons the trainer, before mounting, and after dismounting, should make the horse elevate its head, and bend its head and neck to the right and to the left, as such exercises will aid in the suppling lessons of the mounted horse. To elevate the head of the horse, the trainer will stand in front of the animal, and taking a ring of the bit in each hand, he will, without unnecessary force, extend his arms upward until the neck and head of the horse are raised as high as he can reach. He should then gently lower his arms until the head of the horse comes to a natural position, placing its face about vertically to the ground, and inducing it to yield the lower jaw by gentle plays upon the bit. To bend the head to the left he will stand on the off-side, a little in advance of the shoulder, taking the left rein in his left hand and the right rein in his right hand near the rings on the bit, and he will gently turn the bit in the mouth of the horse so that the head is well turned to the left, the face placed about vertically to the ground by the tension upon both reins, the jaw and neck of the horse being kept free of rigidity by the gentle manner in which the bit is used. In a similar way the head of the horse should be turned to the right, the man standing on the near side in front of the shoulder. These exercises give control over the positions of the head of the horse, and make the neck and jaw supple, so that the animal becomes light and yielding to the reins when it is mounted; and in conducting the bending lessons, the trainer should take care that the head of the horse is held as high as it should be carried when the horse is straight, and in motion under the rider. The young horse must have sufficient exercise, or the trainer will not be able to direct and keep its

CARRYING THE CROUP ABOUT THE FOREHAND.

attention. Many of the disorderly movements, which may become vices, are due to the hysterical condition of the horse. Horses too fresh, and even old trained horses, are difficult to control when nervous from want of work.

3

While the other exercises on foot are being employed, the preliminary lesson for carrying the croup about the forehand may be given. The trainer, standing at the shoulder of the horse, on the near side, and holding the reins under the chin of the horse in his left hand, should give a slight tap of the whip upon the left side, near the girths, so that the horse will take *one* step to the right with the hind legs, the forehand being held in place. This will throw the right fore leg a little in rear of its proper place for the new position, and it will be brought up by a tap of the whip. Then another step will be demanded from the croup, and the right fore leg be again brought up to its place. In this way, step by step, the croup will be made to go about the forehand, the left fore leg acting as a fixed pivot, no step being permitted that is not demanded. In the same manner, the croup will be carried to the left, about the right fore leg as a pivot, the trainer standing at the shoulder on the off-side, and holding the reins under the animal's chin in his right hand, while, with the whip in his left hand, he delivers the taps upon the right flank of the horse.

CHAPTER III

HAND AND HEEL. — THE TROT, THE WALK, CHANGES OF DIRECTION.

THE horse having been taught to go forward freely against a constant light tension upon the reins, it is proper to employ lessons which will confirm its obedience to the combined effects of hands and heels, to demand even and regular paces, and to increase the discipline by which we are to deprive the horse of volition. A brisk, slow trot is the best pace in which to produce these effects; for until the horse is brought to answer every application of the hands and heels, we must have the impulse of a forward movement, upon which the hand may act. A very important rule should be observed in riding; that is, the pressure of the rider's legs, or of his heels, must always precede any action of the hand. I do not now speak of the spur, for that should not be used until the education of the animal is more advanced; and I may say here that the

occasions when the sharp rowel may be applied
to the well-trained horse are very rare, as the
sensitive animal will readily answer the side of
the heel or the pressure of the calf of the leg.   If
the young horse does not answer to the heel, the
demand may be enforced by a light whip-tap
delivered behind the girths.   The snaffle should
still be the bit employed, for while it is only the
exceptional horseman who can get the best effects
in uniting the horse from this simple mouthpiece,
it is less harassing to the young horse than the
curb-bit, and there is still much work that can be
accomplished with it.   The aim of the rider in
the remaining lessons in the snaffle should be to
teach the horse, while it maintains a good bearing, to move in free, even, and regular paces, and
to make the changes of direction smoothly and
correctly.   The rider's heels will bring up impulses which will be directed and controlled by
the hand.   If the mouth has been made a trifle
rigid in teaching the horse to face the bit, it may
now be softened by using gentle tensions upon
'the reins, and by bringing the hind legs of the
animal under the mass by the application of the
rider's heels.   Upon mounting, the rider will draw

the reins until they take a feeling upon the mouth
of the horse. The rider's legs will then be closed
against the flanks, and the hand will make gentle
vibrations of the reins until the head of the horse
is sustained without support, and the mouth gives
elastic response to the hand. The rider will then
know by the movement of the muscles under him
that the impulses are ready, and if the hand gives
sufficient liberty, the horse will move off in a
walk, the rider's legs demanding impulse, and the
hand receiving and directing this impulse. In
the early lessons, the rider should not require too
close a collection in any pace, but the forehand
must not be allowed to get heavy, nor the hind
quarters be permitted to drag. A slightly increased pressure of the rider's heels, enforced by
a whip-tap if necessary, will increase the impulse,
which will be so directed by the hand that the
horse shall quicken its action into the trot. The
speed should not be very great, but the movement
should be clean and strong, the best possible action
in which to cultivate the use of the aids and to
practice the union of the extremities. In this
strong but slow trot the rider should maintain a
regular rate of speed, demanding such collection

as he can without harassing the horse, but always
having in view a clear and even pace. To turn
to the right, the rider will increase the pressure
of his legs upon the flanks, the left leg a little
more strongly than the right, and draw the right
rein sufficiently, while the left measures its effect,
so that the body of the horse will keep true to the
line of the change of direction. When the change
has been effected, the reins will take an even
bearing upon the mouth, and the same state of
collection will be observed as that held before the
change. The change of direction to the left will
be made in exactly the same manner, the right
and left aids being interchanged. To bring the
horse to a walk, the rider's legs should first close
against the animal's flanks, and the tension upon
the reins be increased until the horse reduces the
speed to a walk, when the hand will permit it
liberty to advance in that pace, while the rider's
legs maintain sufficient impulse to insure it being
clear and even. The changes of direction will
be made as in the trot. To bring the horse to a
halt, the rider's legs will first close against the
sides of the horse, and the hand will increase the
tension of the reins until the horse stops, when

first the hand, and then the rider's legs, will cease to act. In increasing or decreasing the speed, the rider's legs will always act before the hand, so that by insuring impulses from the croup, the hand shall always have something with which it may deal. In the walk and in the trot, the horse should be ridden in straight lines, in changes of direction upon circumferences of various diameters, and in figures of eight; and for a few minutes each day the animal should be put into a good brisk trot, as rapid as proves consistent with cadenced action; that is, the impulses from the croup must not be so great as to throw the weight upon the forehand, nor must the forehand be so elevated, or its forces so carried back, as to impede the hind quarters. Whenever fresh impulses are demanded from the croup, the hand must receive them and measure their effects; so in taking the walk from a halt, or the trot from the walk, the hand first relaxes the tension until the impulse is received, and then meets the impulse. In reducing the speed, and in coming to a halt, the rider's heels close against the sides, and the hand increases the tension upon the mouth, until the desired result is obtained, and

the hand ceases to act before the heels are withdrawn from the sides, so that the speed is not
decreased or the halt effected too suddenly, or
followed by an undesired movement backwards.
During all of these lessons, the rider should, by
using gentle vibrations and light tensions upon
the reins, make the mouth of the horse sensitive
and light, his heels carrying the hind legs well
under the mass, so that the horse may have no
reason to hang upon the hand. The horse should
also be made to stand quietly under its rider, and
permit him to make movements and changes of
position while it is. at a halt.

CHAPTER IV.

SUPPLING AND COLLECTING.—THE UNION AND BALANCE OF THE FORCES.

THE resistances of the horse depend upon the rigidity of the muscles of the head, neck and back, whether intentional or due to conformation. When, by cultivating the instinctive actions that follow the application of the bit and spur, we have brought the horse to obey every application of the aids, we can overcome the faults due to the natural conformation by giving an artificial carriage suited to the circumstances, and we can depend upon the animal yielding its will to the demands of the rider. For example, the first impulse of the horse upon the touch of the bit is to yield the jaw; the second impulse is to avoid the restraint and to pull against the bit. We can cultivate the first impulse until the horse instinctively answers the slightest touch of the bit, or we can make the mouth hard and rigid. The first impulse at the touch of the spur is to

carry forward the hind leg of the side upon which
it is applied, and to bend away the croup; the
second impulse would be to spring forward from
the planted hind leg. We can cultivate these
impulses so that we can control the forces of the
croup, and we can demand either one or both of
the impulses. By this cultivation of these instinctive muscular actions which follow the application of the aids, we can readily conquer the
active resistances of the horse, and we can correct
the faults of conformation and carriage to give it
the bearing best suited to controlled movements
under its burthen. A horse at liberty might
move with perfect ease and grace; but when it
bears the weight of a man, and its movements are
checked and impeded by bit and spur, it would be
awkward and constrained in its carriage if the
rider did not arrange the weights and forces to
conform to the new order of affairs. The well-
formed horse requires less aid from the trainer
than the horse of defective structure, but all
horses must submit to an artificial carriage before
they can bear a man safely and smoothly. It is
not every saddle horse that is trained according
to an accepted " method ;" but whether the trainer

knew the fact or not, something of a method was employed before the horse was safe or easy to ride, and it is possible that the horse in self-defence sometimes picks up a proper bearing

ELEVATION OF THE HEAD, MOUNTED.

without the rider being aware of it. Any man who has "broken" a colt must have seen how awkward and rough-paced was the animal at first, and how gradually it acquired a smoother and better balanced mode of moving. The object of

a systematized method is to hasten and perfect
this change from an awkward and unwilling yielding to a quick, even, and ready obedience.

The hand can elevate or depress the forehand
of the horse. The heels can bring forward the
forces of the croup to their highest powers, or
even beyond that point, where they will be domi-
nated by the raised forces of the forehand. Between hand and heel the rider can place the
weights and forces of the extremities where he
wishes. For smooth, even, and regular paces he
will bring the weights and forces into a point so
near that of union and balance that those of the
hind quarters will have such predominance as
will permit the mass to go forward at the desired
rate and pace. A halt will be the result of an
equilibrium of the forces of the extremities. A
retrograde movement will be where the forehand
predominates sufficiently to let the mass move to
the rear. In the same way, either extremity may
be fixed to a spot, and any movement would be
some form of pirouette, or a raising of the other
extremity.

To bring about this union and balance of the
forces, the trainer must not only obtain control

over the forces and weights of the extremities of
the forehand and of the hind quarters, but he
must know how to correct the natural defects of
the animal, so that he can readily produce what

POSITION OF THE HEAD.

he desires. He must reduce the effects of the
stronger parts, and he must strengthen the
powers of the weaker parts. If the horse be high
and well developed in the forehand, and weak and
deficient in the hind quarters, it will be necessary

to have the head carried low enough to permit the forces of the croup to be brought up to a point of balance between them and the forces of the forehand, or the forehand will dominate the croup, or the forces of the croup will be languid, and there will be no unison of action. If the hind quarters be strong and high, and the forehand low and heavy, or weak, the head of the horse must be elevated sufficiently to carry back the forces of the forehand, and the hind legs must be brought under the mass to lower the croup so that the forces of the extremities may be in balance; otherwise the croup will overpower the forehand, and the action of the latter will be dull and cramped.

The form of the animal will suggest to the trainer the exercises best suited to it; and when the rider mounts the horse, he should soon discover what is necessary to bring the forces into the so-called equilibrium. If the horse hangs upon the hand, and is heavy in front, the head should be elevated, and the forces of the forehand be carried back, while the heels bring under the mass the forces of the croup. If the action of the hind quarters is languid, the forehand should be lowered, and the forces of the croup should be stimulated and brought up to the proper point.

When the face of the horse is vertical, the jaw pliant, the spine devoid of rigidity, and the horse

DROPPING HEAD.

seems to grow under the rider, while the action is light, regular, and even, the man should know that the forces are collected and in the best possible position for obtaining perfectly controlled movements. The following exercises are

designed to give the rider power over the forces
of the forehand and of the croup, to enable him to
obtain and preserve this condition, in which the
horse is ready to obey any demand. The trainer
may now put on the double-reined bridle to
accustom the horse to the two bits, but there
should be no curb-chain, and the snaffle only will
be used.

To make the horse elevate the head, the rider will
separate the snaffle-reins, and draw them until he
has a light feeling upon the mouth, closing his
legs against the flanks; he will then raise the
hands so that he takes a light upward pull upon
the reins, and brings the head of the horse as high
as possible, the face parallel with the ground.

From the position described in the foregoing
paragraph, he should bring *the head into position* by gradually dropping the hands and carrying them towards his body with light vibratory
touches upon the reins, slightly pressing the heels
against the flanks to keep the horse up to the bit.
When the horse curves the crest, and brings the
face about vertical to the ground, the jaw being
pliant and the head not too low, the rider should
release the tension upon the reins to reward the
horse.

To make the horse lower the head, the rider should take a light feeling upon the mouth, with his legs closed against the flanks; the hand should then be held low and a steady tension

BENDING THE HEAD, MOUNTED.

taken upon the reins: the moment the horse lowers the head, the hand should release the tension upon the reins, the legs be withdrawn from the flanks, and the animal should be rewarded. Then by another tension upon the

reins, made in the same manner, the head should
be still further depressed, and this obedience
acknowledged. By degrees, the horse can be
taught to lower the head until the nose reaches
the ground.

To assist in making the whole neck and the
jaw supple, the rider should *bend the head first to
one side, and then to the other*, until 'the horse can
be brought to carry the face to the rear without
rigidity or resistance. To make this bend, say to
the left, the rider will put the horse perfectly
straight, the face vertical to the ground, and the
head carried at a natural height. Then the
snaffle-reins being held divided in the two hands,
he should close his legs against the flanks, the
right leg a little more strongly than the left, and
by gentle tensions upon the left rein, supported
and governed by the right rein, he will give the
head of the horse a slight bend to the left. The
object of the rider will be to obtain this by as
light tension upon the reins as will produce the
bend, and he should keep the head at the proper
height, the face vertical to the ground, and the
under jaw of the horse elastic and supple: gradually the bend, will be made until the face looks to

the rear. The rider will always carry back the head to the position straight with the body by means of the reins, not permitting the horse to volunteer this. In the same manner, and with

CARRYING THE HIND LEGS UNDER THE BODY.

the same care, the head and neck shall be bent to the right, right and left aids being interchanged.

The rider should occasionally make the horse *carry its hind legs under the body* by closing both heels against the flanks and giving light whip-taps upon the rump, holding the forehand in place.   To bring the horse into a natural position, the hind legs should not be permitted to move to the rear, but the trainer should induce the horse

CARRYING THE HIND LEGS UNDER THE BODY.

to advance the fore legs until the horse rests easily.

Should the mounted horse be slow in learning this, a few lessons given on foot will soon show it what the trainer demands.   Standing on the near side, and holding the snaffle-reins in the left hand under the horse's chin, the man should apply the whip in light strokes upon the rump ; as soon as a hind leg is carried under the body the horse should be rewarded, and the lesson then be resumed, and the other hind leg be brought up. In time the horse, mounted or unmounted, can be made to carry both hind legs well under its body.

When the mounted horse will answer readily the combined applications of the whip and of the heels, the whip taps should be dispensed with, and the hind legs should be carried under the mass at the pressure of the rider's heels, while the hand gently keeps the forehand in place.

CHAPTER V.

THE exercises described in this chapter may be conducted in the snaffle-bridle, or in the double bridle without the curb-chain, the rider using the snaffle-reins. The lessons will be begun by practice in some of the preceding exercises, particularly in those in which the horse shows the least improvement, and the animal should be ridden in the walk and in the trot, but not to the point of fatigue. I may say here that it is an excellent practice to put the young horse, even after it has been placed in the double bridle, through the whole course of lessons from the beginning.

The reversed pirouette is a movement in which the horse carries the croup about the forehand, the outer fore leg acting as a fixed pivot; that is, if the croup is carried about to the right, the left fore leg will remain upon the ground, and the body will go about it, the other legs taking such steps as to insure the movement being made smoothly and lightly. The reversed pirouette

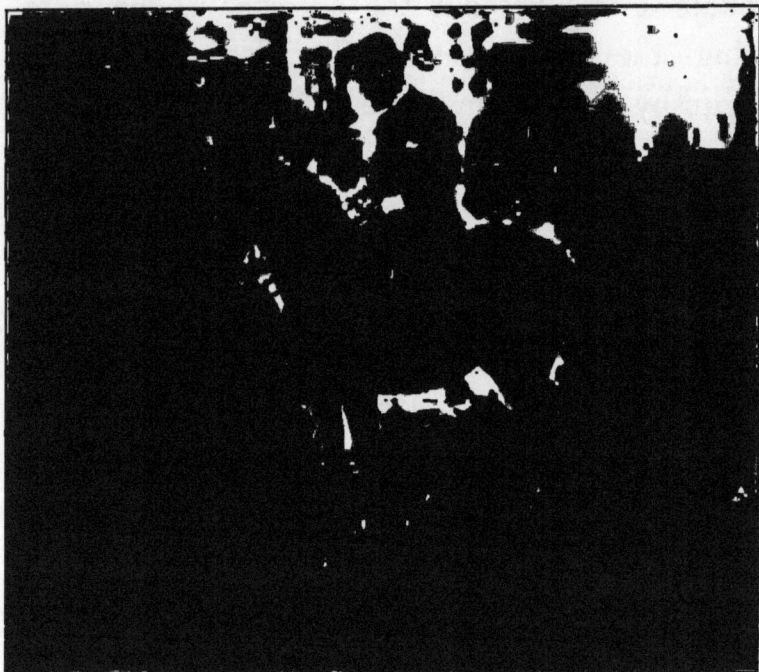

REVERSED PIROUETTE.

prepares the horse for the gallop and the gallop change, supples and makes obedient the hind quarters, and is most useful generally in the education of the animal. To teach this to the horse, say to the right, the rider will bring it to a halt,

and demand some degree of union of the extremities by a pressure of the legs against the flanks,
and a light tension upon the reins ; he will then
bend the head slightly to the right, by an increased
tension upon the right rein measured by the left
rein, and increase the pressure of the left heel
until the croup takes one step to the right, the
forehand held in place.   If the horse volunteers
more steps, it will be stopped by the right heel of
the rider.   Upon its taking the step to the right,
the rider shall reward the horse by withdraw-
ing the aids.   The horse should then again be
collected, be made to take a second step, and then
be stopped and rewarded.   In time it should be
made to make the complete circle of the croup,
step by step, about the forehand, the head bent
to the right, the left fore leg in place as a pivot,
and the whole horse light and without rigidity.
The short steps of the right fore leg should be
induced by a vibration of the right rein, and if
necessary, the rider may tap the right fore leg
with the whip, to insure its being brought up as
the position of the mass changes.   Should the
horse not answer the left heel readily, its indication may be enforced by the rider carrying his

right hand behind his back, and tapping the horse with the whip upon the left side, just behind the girths.

The pirouette reversed to the left should be made in the same way, right and left aids being

APPLYING WHIP TO THE NEAR FLANK.

interchanged. If the whip is used to teach the indication of the right heel in bending the croup to the left, it should be held in the rider's right hand, with the tip down, and be applied just behind the girths, as the right heel is giving its pressure. These pirouettes reversed should be made from the halt, until the horse is put into the double bridle, and the rider should insist upon as much lightness and regularity as he can demand.

The *low pirouette* is an exercise for disciplining the forehand, and in preparing the animal for the pirouettes in action. In the low pirouette the forehand is carried about the croup at the walk, the inner hind leg acting as the pivot, the outer hind leg being moved sufficiently, as the horse turns, to keep its proper place, with regard to the changing positions of the mass; the head of the horse should be slightly bent in the direction of the movement. To teach the movement, say to the right, the horse should be united between hand and heels; the head of the horse should then be slightly bent to the right, and the forehand moved about the croup by the action of the reins, the increased tension upon the right rein being measured by the left, the left leg of the rider holding the croup in place, and inducing the movement of the left hind leg of the horse; when the half-circle has been made,

the horse should be put straight in the new
position and rewarded.

The low pirouette to the left may be made in
the same manner, the right and left aids being

LOW PIROUETTE.

interchanged, the head of the horse slightly bent
to the left, the left hind leg being the pivot.

The horse should also be practised in bending
the head to the right and to the left, while in the
walk, upon direct lines, and upon circumferences

of circles. As a rule, this bend should not be
very great, as the rider must avoid teaching the
horse to throw its head too far to either side; but
the forehand must be so supple that, should the
rider require it, he can turn the head so far that
the horse looks to the rear. The horse must not
be permitted to volunteer the bend, or to bend
further than is demanded, or to carry the head
back to the line of progress, but the whole of the
forehand should be under the rider's control, and
the jaw should be light and elastic, and every
tension upon one rein must have its effect measured and controlled by the other rein; that is,
in such demands for bends and turns, there
should always be a tension upon both reins, the
acting rein having the stronger tension, the other
rein guarding against too great an effect of the
acting rein.

We have now but one exercise remaining for
the snaffle, the movement upon two paths, the
forehand on one path slightly in advance of the
croup upon a parallel path, the head slightly bent
in the direction of progress. When, in changing
direction in this movement, the forehand follows
the outer path of the greater circumference, we

have *the travers.* When the croup follows the path of the greater circumference at the turns and changes of direction, we have *the renvers;* that is, in the riding house, "the head to the

TRAVERS.

wall" upon two paths is *travers*, "the croup to the wall" is *renvers*.

To teach the movement upon two paths, say to the right, the rider will take the horse well united in a walking pace, with a wall on the left hand: then he will slightly bend the head to the

right, and increase the pressure of his left heel
against the flank, until the horse moves sideways,
with its body placed diagonally across the line of
movement, the forehand a little in advance of the
croup, the left leg of each extremity passing in
front of the right leg. At first, the rider should
be content with a few steps to the side, and then
he should straighten the horse and let it proceed
for a short time on a direct single path. To
make the turn in travers, the croup will be retarded upon a small circle, while the forehand is
carried about the larger outside circle, so that,
when the change of direction has been made, the
horse will be in the proper position with reference
to the two paths. By gradually extending the
lessons, the horse should be brought to go any
required distance in travers, the horse being light
and without rigidity or resistance in any part,
and being kept well up to the lines. The travers
to the left may be made in the same manner,
right and left aids being interchanged. Head to
the wall should be well practised before the rider
undertakes croup to the wall or renvers, as in the
latter movement the rider does not have, to so
great an extent, the assistance of the wall in controlling the position of the horse. As the aids

are used in exactly the same manner in both movements, the lessons in travers prepare the animal for the renvers.

To make the horse perform the renvers, say to the left, the rider will take the animal in a united

RENVERS.

walk on a single path about half its length from the wall, which will be on his left hand, then by bending its head slightly to the left, and by increasing the pressure of the right heel, he will induce the horse to pass along on two paths, the

forehand a little in advance of the croup, which
will be, by the bend given it, close to the wall,
and in a measure guided by it. In changing
direction in renvers, the forehand will be retarded
upon the inner smaller circle, while the croup
goes about on the outer larger circumference, the
horse holding its proper position to the two lines,
at every point, during the turn, so that the body
will be diagonally disposed across the lines when
the change has been made and the new direction
is followed.

Great care should be taken in the exercise
upon the two paths that the position of the
horse, its suppleness and elasticity, and its regularity of pace are observed; as much of the
precision and promptness with which all other
movements may be made are dependent upon the
discipline exacted in travers and renvers.

It should now be a very easy matter to perfect
the training of the horse. We have passed the
stage where resistances are to be expected; we
should have the horse fairly suppled and obedient
to the aids, with a lightness and vivacity that
gives a very different bearing from that we found
in the timorous and awkward colt; and when, in
the double bridle, we can bring about the various

forms of balance and union of the forces, the rider may demand and secure any movement or action of which the animal is physically capable.

After the horse has been taught to pass "in head to the wall," and "in croup to the wall," smoothly and regularly, it should be made to perform travers and renvers away from the wall, when the rider must depend wholly upon the hand and the heels. In these movements to either hand upon two paths, the shoulder of the rider upon the side of the movement should be slightly retired : that is, in travers or renvers to the right, the right shoulder of the rider should be retired ; in travers or renvers to the left, the left shoulder should be retired.

There is a movement practised in most armies called *schlissen*, or "closing up," in which the horse is made to pass to the right or to the left upon two paths, with the body straight across the line of direction ; but this is objectionable by reason that the horse is apt to knock its legs. Intervals can be readily closed by the oblique movements, and awkward interferences of the horse's legs are avoided.

5

Part II.

IN THE DOUBLE-REINED BRIDLE.

CHAPTER I.

FROM this time forth the complete double-
reined bridle should be used, the curb-chain
so arranged that it will fit into the chin groove
without pinching, and yet not so loose that
the effect of the lever is diminished. The curb-
chain should never be changed to give a lighter
or a stronger effect to the bit; but any desired
changes in the powers of the curb-bit should be
by the use of long or short branches. For the
ordinary purposes with horses of normal jaws
a bit with branches measuring four and one-
half inches from the middle of the mouth-piece
to the fitting of the lower ring should be found
to answer.

The curb-bit is a lever which acts upon the
bare bars of the lower jaw of the horse, and
gives the rider greater power in certain ways
over the animal than the snaffle, which does

not always take its bearing upon the most
sensitive points; but the latter has a wider
range of effect than the curb-bit, and should
be used with it to assist the stronger instrument
when it fails by reason of its limits. The curb-
bit is of use in restraining and in carrying back
the impulses. The snaffle is of use in elevating
or in depressing the forehand, and in teaching
the changes of direction.

The trainer should consider the two extremities of the horse as parts of a machine which
should be made to work in unison. The rider's
heels control the hind quarters and bring up
the impulses. The hand controls the forehand
and directs the mass, which has been united
between the application of the aids. The forces
of the extremities should be united as closely
and be kept as level as is consistent with the
movement which the rider desires to obtain.

When a horse moves along in a shambling
pace, bearing upon the hand or dragging its
hind quarters, it is dis-united, and is in no condition to give quick and ready obedience to its
rider, or even to bear him with safety. Should
the rider demand increased impulses from the

croup and meet these with the hand until the cadence of the pace becomes regular, and the animal moves with its head held perpendicularly to the plane of movement, its neck curved,

IN HAND IN THE TROT.

its mouth supple, and taking just such a tension upon the reins as permits the indications of the reins to be given, the horse is " in hand," the state in which the animal should habitually be ridden.

A still closer collection is "the union," in which the forces are so nearly balanced that the pace is very slow and the increased exertion of the horse is turned into action. It is best taught from a slow trot, the impulses from the croup in that pace giving the hand the means of bringing about the close collection of the forces. When the crest is curved, the jaw is pliant, and the muscles of the neck swell and play, and the horse seems to grow under the rider, while the pace is one in which with bold and high action each pair of diagonally disposed legs work in perfect unison, the horse then is in "the union," the highest form of collection consistent with motion in which there is no pause at each stride. The union may also be produced in the gallop, where the pace will be one of four beats. The union is used in reducing the speed for changes of direction, as preliminary for the half-halt, and for the production of brilliant action.

When the forces are brought to a point of absolute union and balance under the rider there can be no motion, and we have the *half-halt* or *poise*. The horse is still in action, that is, the legs are flexed; but there is a momentary pause brought about by bringing back the forces of the forehand until they meet in balance the acting forces of the croup. From

UNITED TROT.

this poise the horse may be moved to the front, to the rear, or to either side, while the animal is still light, by the aids making some demand before the flexed legs are planted. As this half-halt requires great nervous and muscular exertion, it can only be sustained for the moment, and the horse must either make some movement, or grow heavy or disorderly. The half-halt is employed in teaching the gallop changes, in making marked changes of directions, as in the pirouettes direct and reversed, and in bringing the horse to a finished halt from action. There may be intermediate forms of collection; but the three we have fixed upon have their uses and their distinctive peculiarities. For example, if the forces are more closely collected than "the union," we should have a pause in each stride, as is the case in the "passage;" or if the forces are less closely collected than in "the union," we might have more action than when "in hand," but lose the brilliancy and the bold strides of "the union."

"In hand" is, therefore, the lowest form of collection in which we can have suppleness and clear even paces.

"The union" is where we have the closest collection compatible with uninterrupted motion.

"The poise" is a half-halt, produced by bringing the forces of the extremities to a point of union and balance, and can be maintained for a moment only, when some movement should be demanded, while the legs are flexed, or the horse should be permitted to come to a finished halt and the aids be withdrawn.

HALF-HALT FROM THE TROT.

These different forms of collection should be practised in the walk, in the trot, in the gallop, and at the halt. As has been said, it is easier to produce them from the trot than from either the halt, or the other paces, as the trot is a level gait in which the strong and regular impulses assist the aids in uniting the horse. But the rider should be able to bring the horse "in hand in place" after one or two lessons in

IN HAND IN PLACE.

the curb-bit, and in time he will be able to demand the closer collections without the impulses of the paces. The horse should always be brought *in hand in place* before any movement is required. The closer forms of collection at the halt may be practised simply for the discipline they involve.

It should be borne in mind that the tension upon the curb-reins should never be long-continued or severe; the bridle-hand should give vibratory plays upon the mouth, so that it will be kept fresh and elastic, ready to yield to any demand of the reins, and never forced to a rigid resistance for a defence against a cruel use of the bit. When the horse has been so disciplined that it instinctively gives up all opposition to the bit, the animal cannot rear, bolt, or refuse to turn. When it has been so disciplined that it instinctively answers to the spur, a more difficult task, the rider's will is paramount in everything.

CHAPTER II.

INDIRECT INDICATIONS OF THE CURB-BIT. —
IN THE DOUBLE BRIDLE.

THE trained horse should be ridden with the reins held in one hand, the other being free, to assist the bridle-hand or for any other purpose. It will be necessary to teach the horse to obey the touches of the curb-rein upon the neck, or the *indirect indications* of the curb-bit, as we may call them, so that the bridle-hand may control the movements of the horse without the aid of the snaffle, which up to this time has been the bit in which the horse has been trained.

The trainer must see that the horse understands and obeys the *direct* as well as the *indirect* indications of the curb-bit, for they are not incompatible, and it will be safer for the latter to be preceded by a slight suggestion of the *direct* touch of the bit in the manner I shall hereafter explain.

In teaching the indirect indications of the curb-bit, I have found the following manner of holding the reins very efficient: the curb-reins held in the left hand divided by the little finger, the loose ends of the reins carried through the hand, and held fast by the thumb against the forefinger; the hand held high or low as the horse requires the head to be elevated or lowered, the thumbs pointing towards the horse's ears. The right hand, carried above the left, should hold the snaffle-reins, and when it is necessary to employ the latter, the left hand will release the tension upon the curb-reins, the tension upon the curb-reins being resumed when the snaffle ceases to act; that is, there should not be a tension upon both sets of reins at the same time.

If the exercises described in the preceding chapters have been carefully carried out, the rider should experience no difficulty in bringing the horse to the various forms of collection with the curb-reins, particularly if he bears in mind that the impulses from action help the aids in uniting the extremities of the horse.

To turn the horse to the right, the right snaffle-rein, supported and its effects measured by the left snaffle-rein, will begin the turn; and as soon as the head bends in the new direction, the left hand will be carried to the right so that the left curb-rein will take a tension against the left side of the neck of the horse; this interposition of the neck will give to the curb-bit an indication similar to the direct tension upon the snaffle-rein. As soon as the change has been effected, the snaffle-reins will straighten the horse, and the even tension upon the curb-reins will be resumed.

In the same way the turn to the left will be begun by the left snaffle-rein, supported and its effects measured by the right snaffle-rein, and then the left hand will be carried to the left until the right curb-rein takes a tension against the right side of the neck of the horse. The snaffle-reins will straighten the horse after the change of direction has been made, and then the even tensions upon the curb-reins will be resumed.

Of course, in these, and in all other changes of direction upon single lines, the horse will first be prepared by a closer collection, and the outside heel will keep the croup upon the path followed by the forehand.

In the walk and in the trot, the horse should be made to change direction in this manner, and to pass in circles of various diameters and in various figures, the same principles being observed. Gradually the introductory direct indication of the snaffle-reins may be reduced and finally be dispensed with, the curb-reins alone being used in changing direction, when the curb-reins should be employed in the following manner: still held in the left hand, the thumb pointing towards the ears of the horse, the snaffle-reins held loosely in the left hand, divided by the long finger, or in the right hand, as the rider elects. To turn to the right, the bridle-hand will be turned so that the thumb points to the rider's right shoulder, which gives a direct indication of the right curb-rein; the bridle-hand is then carried to the right so that the left curb-rein has a tension against the left side of the horse's neck, which gives an indication similar in effect to that already made by the right curb-rein. When the change of direction has been made, the hand should be dropped, and an even tension taken upon the two curb-reins.

To turn to the left, the left hand should be

turned so that the thumb points towards the
ground over the left shoulder of the horse; this
gives a direct tension upon the left curb-rein.
The hand should then be carried to the left, so
that the right curb-rein takes a tension against
the right side of the horse's neck, which will give
an indication similar in effect to that made by the
direct tension upon the left curb-rein. When the
change of direction has been effected, the hand
should be placed in position, and an even tension
taken upon the two curb-reins.

By a little practice, the horse may be taught to
elevate or to depress the head by means of the
curb-reins in exactly the same manner as with
the snaffle-reins; and this practice is essential, as
a thoroughly trained horse should be managed
by the curb-bit independently of the snaffle,
although it is always safe to have the latter, in
case, through lack of discipline, the horse fails to
obey the curb-bit in the points where its effects
are the weakest.

I wish to say here that I have never seen a
" combination bit" that could supply the place
of curb and snaffle. To properly control the
saddle-horse, one must have the effects of the

snaffle, — the best bit, and perhaps the most ancient mouth-piece made of metal, — and he should have the curb-bit in connection with it. If a single bit is used it should be the snaffle, and never the other alone. I do not dispute that many of the patent bits may be of value for harness-horses, but they are worthless for the rider; and the Pelham bit, which has for many years been widely employed, does not give either of the two principal effects for which it was designed.

CHAPTER III.

THE GALLOP. — THE GALLOP CHANGES.

I DO not put my horses into the gallop until they have been thoroughly disciplined in the walk and in the trot in the various forms of collection. It is then a very simple thing to teach a horse to gallop with true action in an even cadence.

In the gallop, a horse goes into air from a fore leg in each stride; it then plants the hind leg of the opposite side, then the other hind leg, then the fore leg of the side of the first planted hind leg, and finally the remaining fore leg, from which it again goes into air. In this pace, the legs of one side take advanced steps in each stride, and if these be the right legs, the horse is in gallop right, and if they be the left legs the horse is in gallop left; that is, in gallop right the horse plants the left hind leg after going into air; it then plants the right hind leg, then the left fore leg, and lastly the right fore leg, from which it goes into air for a new stride.

The horse should be in gallop right in turning to the right, in gallop left in turning to the left, so that it will have a bearer under the centre of gravity as the turn is made.

The gallop is called a pace of four beats, but in the ordinary slow gallop in hand, the second planted hind leg and the opposite fore leg strike the ground so nearly at the same moment, that it becomes a pace of three beats. In the school-gallop, or shortened gallop, the forehand is so supported that the second planted hind leg comes to the ground an appreciable time before the diagonally disposed fore leg, and the pace is of four distinct beats. In the rapid gallop the horse is so much extended, that we have again an example of four beats.

A horse takes the gallop when the weights have been shifted so violently that the balance necessary for the other paces is impossible; in the gallop the legs are brought to the ground one after another, and no matter how great may be the changes in the position of the centre of gravity, the pace can be maintained as long as the horse can stand up.

The horse goes into the gallop by taking the weights upon the forehand, and by then carrying one of the hind legs under the centre of gravity, when it is in some form of the gallop.

The horse is false in the gallop if it turn to the right in gallop left, or to the left in gallop right, unless the movement be intentional on the part of the rider, when it is called the contra gallop. It is also false in the gallop if the forehand has gallop right (or left), and the croup has gallop left (or right); that is, a cross gallop.

To teach the horse to take *gallop right*, the rider should collect the animal in a very slow trot; he should then increase the pressure of the left heel, and make a gentle upward play with the right rein. These indications of the aids will demand the necessary impulse, induce the proper disposition of the hind legs, and lighten the right side of the forehand, so that, as the left hind leg is carried under the centre of gravity, the horse will go into gallop right. When the horse takes the gallop, the aids must maintain the action, and the animal should be put straight upon the line of progress. The rate should not be so rapid that the horse cannot be kept in

hand, or so slow and languid that the animal
will be disposed to resume the trot. The upward play of the direct rein should not be too
marked, and it must be supported by the opposite

BREAK INTO GALLOP FROM SLOW TROT.

rein, so that the head will not be displaced. In
the early lessons, the croup will of necessity be
somewhat bent, but as the lessons progress, the
horse must be taught to take the gallop without
a perceptible bend of the croup.

To teach the horse to take the gallop left, the right heel will demand the proper position of the hind legs, and the impulses from the croup, and an upward play of the left rein will prepare the fore legs for the proper stride; the rider's left leg supporting his right leg as it gives the stronger pressure, the right rein measuring the effects of the direct rein. Of course, what has been said about putting and keeping the horse straight in the gallop right applies equally here.

After the horse will take and maintain either gallop right or gallop left, in a free and even pace, the rider should carefully practise bringing it to the shortened-gallop (or school-gallop), by demanding a closer union; and, in time, from this shortened-gallop to the "poise," or "half-halt," resuming the gallop before the animal has grown heavy in hand, and gradually making the half-halt (what it should be) nothing more than a "rest of one beat" in the cadence of the pace.

When the horse has been taught to observe the half-halt, it may be taught to take gallop right and gallop left from "in place" in exactly the same manner as from the walk or from the slow trot.

The horse should have long and carefully conducted lessons in the gallop, being made to
change the rates of speed and the forms of collection at the will of the rider; and it should be
made to gallop in circles of various diameters,
first with the legs of the side to which it is turning making the extended strides, and afterwards
in the contra gallop.

The horse should then be ready to be taught
the *gallop changes.* I have said that the horse
goes into air from a fore leg at each stride, this
fore leg being the right in gallop right, the left in
gallop left. It is when the hind legs are leaving
the ground for the weight to be thrown upon this
advanced fore leg, that the opportunity is given
the hind legs to change their order, and when the
fore legs are free from the ground they change
their order, and the change is made in one stride
without either extremity being false; that is, in
changing from gallop right to gallop left, the
hind legs will change their order (so that the
right hind leg will first be planted, and then
the left hind leg, which has passed it, in advance
of it), when they are free from the ground in
some stride, the forehand having the weights;

and as soon as the right fore leg is free from the ground, it will be advanced and be again planted, and then the left fore leg will be advanced and brought to the ground, the horse going into air for a new stride from the latter.

To teach the horse to change from gallop right to gallop left, the animal should be put into a very slow gallop right on a straight line. After some strides in this pace, the rider will bring the horse to a slow trot for half a dozen strides, and then very quietly, and without harassing or exciting the horse, put it into gallop left, by collecting the animal, by slightly retiring his left shoulder, applying the right leg, and making an upward play with the left rein.

Gradually these strides in the trot will be reduced in number, and in time be replaced by a half-halt between the gallop right and gallop left, the aids to make the change from the half-halt being applied gently but with exactness; and the shoulder of the rider upon the side of the new change being slightly retired, so that his weight will be properly disposed. The half-halt will then be reduced until the horse makes the change from gallop right to gallop left in the beat of the pace, the horse being closely collected in a very slow gallop, and the increased pressure of the rider's right leg and the upward play of the left rein taking effect at the moment the

GALLOP RIGHT.

advanced hind leg gives its impulse in some stride. In very rapid gallops the horse must have the idea of changing before the advanced fore leg (in the old stride) is brought to the ground; but the rider cannot with certainty

demand the gallop changes at a high rate of
speed ; and in the gallop, where changes may be
produced, the principal impulse in each leap
comes from the hind leg on the side of the
advanced fore leg, and it is as this impulse is
being given, that the effects of the aids for
demanding the change should be felt.

During these lessons in changing from gallop
right to gallop left, a similar method should be
followed in teaching the changes from left to
right, both changes being taught in the same
order ; that is, both sides of the horse should be
equally practised in the lessons with the trotting
strides between the changes, and in the lessons
with the half-halt between the changes, and in
the lessons where the changes are made in the
· beat of the pace.

To produce the changes smoothly and evenly,
the trainer must be satisfied with very slow progress : the slight motions of the rider's body
being gently made, and the aids applied neither
abruptly nor roughly.

After the horse will make the changes perfectly at any desired stride upon straight lines,
the rider should practise the changes in gallop in

turning from a circle on one hand to a circle on the other hand, taking care that the change is made as the turn to the other hand is demanded; for, in turning abruptly from a circle on one

GALLOP CHANGES.   FROM RIGHT TO LEFT.

hand to a circle on the other, the horse will often try to begin the change with the fore legs, and this is not only a false movement, but it is dangerous, as there would be no support under the centre of gravity in making the turn.   Of course this objection holds good for the contra gallop, but that when made intentionally is made with care, and by giving it something of the character of the renvers the rider may reduce the risk.

It will be a mere matter of skill and practice to make the gallop changes at any stride, or even at every stride.

It is important that the body of the horse should be kept straight in both gallops, and the bend of the horse in making the changes should be imperceptible; the motions of the rider's body as he retires the right shoulder for gallop right, the left shoulder for gallop left, should also be slight, the seat from the waist to the knees being undisturbed, and with a little practice he can shift the weights by muscular movements in such a manner that he will not have the appearance of having changed his position. The less obvious the motions of the rider in controlling the horse, the higher will be his skill.

The *contra gallop*, that is, turning to the right in gallop left, to the left in gallop right, should often be practised during the lesson in the gallop changes, so that the horse shall not volunteer an undesired change when a turn happens to be made. Until the horse becomes clever on its feet, these changes of direction in the contra gallop may be made in renvers (upon two paths) as the horse will be less apt to fall in the event of a mistake.

CHAPTER IV.

TROT AND GALLOP. — TRAVERS AND RENVERS. —
PIROUETTES FROM ACTION. — LOW PIROUETTES.
— THE PIROUETTE VOLTE.

THE horse should now be ridden in the travers
and renvers in the walk and in the united
trot, both to the right and to the left, upon
straight lines and upon circles, half-circles, and
other figures, changing from travers to renvers
and from renvers to travers, the proper bend of
the head being always demanded, and the diagonal position of the body of the horse with reference to the parallel paths being observed. In
turning from travers to renvers, or from renvers
to travers, large circles should at first be followed,
to be gradually reduced until the movement
becomes a low pirouette, or a pirouette reversed,
the horse having been very closely collected for
abrupt changes of direction.

In riding the horse in the shortened, or united
trot, a very high state of union and balance

should be demanded, the increased action taking place under the horse, the pairs of diagonally disposed legs working in perfect unison, and the horse being supple throughout. In all the side movements in this trot the leg of the rider which demands the movement should give accentuated pressure as the fore leg of the opposite side is being raised and extended, in order that the diagonal action may be obtained and sustained by the movement of the hind leg on the side of the acting heel; it being understood that the other heel of the rider always measures and controls the effect of the heel giving the accentuated pressure.

At first, the snaffle-reins must assist those of the curb-bit in demanding these movements upon two parallel paths; but the use of the former will be gradually dispensed with in the manner before described : the indirect indications of the curb-rein being always preceded by a tension upon the direct curb-rein. That is, in bending the head to the right to pass to the right, the bridle-hand will be turned towards the rider's right shoulder, to give a direct tension upon the right curb-rein, and then carried over to the right so the left curb-rein will be brought against the neck of the horse : in bending to the left to pass to the left, the bridle-hand will be turned so that the thumb points to the ground over the left shoulder of the horse, and it should then be carried to the left, so that the right rein will take a tension with the right side of the horse's neck intervening.

While upon single direct lines in the united trot, the horse should be practised in the reversed pirouettes from that pace.

If, in the united trot, the horse be passing upon a single straight line, and it be desired to move in the opposite direction, the rider will bring the animal to the half-halt, bend the head slightly to the right and fix the forehand in place, while his left leg carries the croup about to the right in the beat of the trot: when the reversed pirouette is so far made that the horse faces in the new direction, the animal will be put straight, the balance between the forces be resumed by a reduced tension upon the reins and by demanding renewed impulses from the croup (which must be met and measured by the hand), and the horse will go back upon the path by which it came in the same form of trot, without having grown heavy or disunited. The reversed pirouette left will be made in a similar manner, by carrying the croup about to the left, the head bent to the left.

PIROUETTE VOLTE.

All of this work upon two paths, in the walk and in the trot, prepares the horse for the pirouette volte, the most important movement for the mounted soldier that we can obtain from the horse. The trooper who can wheel his horse in the gallop has a less skilled adversary at a great disadvantage; and in everything connected with the mounted soldier, the bridle-hand makes the sword hand effective or of no avail.

For the galloping movements upon two paths, the pace should either be the school gallop or a slow gallop of three beats.

After the horse is fairly well accustomed to pass on straight lines, and to make the ordinary changes of direction of 90° in the travers gallop, it should be brought to make the travers in the gallop, to either hand, upon the whole circles of large diameters, gradually reducing these. The work upon the circles should not be continued for any length of time at any one lesson, and the circles should not be much reduced too rapidly, or the horse will become heavy and constrained in action.

The diameters of the circumferences about which these movements in the travers in gallop are made will in time be reduced, until the croup passes about a circle so small that the inner hind foot treads on a central spot, and we shall have the *pirouette volte.*

The demi-pirouette volte will then be demanded

from the gallop on a single path in a straight line in the following manner. The horse being in, say gallop right, the rider, on reaching the point where the turn is to be made, will demand a half-halt, retire his right shoulder, throw back the weights to keep the croup in place, carry the forehand about, and resume the gallop back over the line upon which the horse has just passed. By practice, the half-halt can be so much reduced as to be barely perceptible, and the pirouette volte will be made almost in the beat of the pace.

The full pirouette volte to the right is made in the same manner, except that the turn is completed, and the horse is brought in a series of gallop strides, the inner hind leg treading in the centre of the circle about which the body turns, to face in the original direction.

By a similar means, right and left aids being interchanged, the demi-pirouette volte and the full pirouette volte will be made to the left from gallop left.

The horse should also be made to pass in circles in the gallop in renvers, the head towards the centre, the forehand, slightly retarded, upon the inner circumference.

Whenever, in the gallop upon the two paths an abrupt turn or change of direction is to be made, the horse should be brought to a *half-halt*, and if the turn requires a change in the gallop (from right to left or from left to right), the gallop change should be effected when the half-halt is made; for it must be borne in mind that in passing to the right the gallop must be right, in passing to the left the gallop must be left.

For example, if the horse be in travers gallop to the left, and it is desired to go back over the same lines, in travers (or in renvers) left, at the point where the turn is to be made the rider will bring the horse to a half-halt, throw back the forces to fix and hold the croup, carry the forehand about to the left until the body of the horse is properly placed with regard to the changed direction, and resume the gallop left upon two paths in the direction whence the horse has come. Or, if the horse be in the gallop left upon two parallel paths, and it is desired to pass back in gallop right over the same lines, the rider, upon coming to the point where the change of direction is to be made, will bring the horse to a half-halt, change from gallop left to gallop right, throw back the forces to fix and hold the croup, carry the forehand over to the right, so that the body of the horse will be properly placed across the parallel paths, and pass to the right, in travers (or in renvers) in gallop right.

CHAPTER V.

THE UNION WITHOUT THE REINS.

WITH every horseman there may be occasions when it will be important that his bridle-hand should be free, and that he should be

UNION WITHOUT REINS.

able to depend upon his horse maintaining the speed, action, and union, of the moment in which the tension upon the reins is released. It is also excellent discipline, on general principles, to ac-

UNION WITHOUT REINS. GALLOP.

custom the horse to move in a regularly cadenced pace, without the support of the hand.

This union without support can be readily taught a horse which has been brought to carry itself in the various forms of collection, by dropping the hand for a moment when the horse is in hand, or more closely united, and resuming the tension upon the reins before the animal loses its lightness or has increased its speed, the rider's heels acting before the tension upon the reins is resumed, to insure the impulses. This momentary dropping of the hand will be exchanged by gradual steps for longer periods of unsupport, until the horse, once in hand or more closely united, will hold its state of collection and maintain the same speed for an appreciable time. The lessons should first be given in the shortened trot, and when the horse is thoroughly disciplined at that pace, it may be taught in the same manner to move without support in the gallop. I have schooled horses, without any great labor, to make the gallop changes with the reins loose upon the neck, by bringing the horse to observe the half-halt without support when the body of the rider was bent backwards, and by gently giving the indications for the change with the spur at the moment the half-halt was made.

CHAPTER VI.

THE too constant use of the spurs will deaden the sensibilities of the horse, and render it dull and sluggish. Every saddle horse should be taught to bear the attacks of the spur with complacency, but the occasions when the sharp rowel is required on a well-trained horse are very rare. The schooling of a horse renders it quick and vivacious; some horses show so much mettle and life that their obedience appears wonderful to the uninitiated; yet that very vivacity is one of the results of schooling, and the animal is taught to be ready to obey the most gently given demand with precision and alacrity. The mare which I rode for the illustrations of the advanced lessons in this book, shows quick and vigorous movements; but she has not been touched with the spur three times since she was taught to bear its

attacks, and she is now at least fifteen years
old.

The best time for teaching the horse to bear
the spur is during the early lessons in the double-
reined bridle; for by that time the animal has
learned something of the indications of the
rider's heels, and should have great confidence
in its trainer. On some occasion when the hind
quarters require stimulating, the rider should
give a slight scratch with the rowel of one
spur, and then calm the horse if it shows sur-
prise or excitement. Later, it should, under
similar circumstances, be given a slight scratch
with the other spur, and again be calmed.
Gradually it should be taught to take the spur
attacks, first of one spur, and then of both
together, with the same complacency with
which it bore the pressure of the bare heels;
the opportunity for doing this can be found
in the exercises on two paths, and in those
for demanding the various forms of collection.
After the horse has been taught to receive
the spur attacks quietly, the aid may be applied
by pressing the side of the heel against the
flank of the horse, and the spur-scratch should

be given only when the severer form of the aid seems to be required. The spur should never be used with force, or in punishment.

It is highly important that horses which are to be employed in the cavalry, should be taught to come to an immediate halt, even from high rates of speed. This can be effected without danger of injury to the animal, if the proper precautions are observed. The theory is, that when the hind legs are carried in under the mass, in any stride, the forehand is raised and its forces are carried back, while the weights and the returned momentum are received by the hind legs when they are in the best position for taking the shock.

It is a very simple matter to teach the horse to come to a finished halt in any gallop stride, and all of the lessons in collecting are preparatory for it; but it should not be practised until the animal has been thoroughly trained in everything recommended in the preceding chapter, as the rider requires the fullest obedience.

The rider should first practise the horse in coming to a halt from the walk (the horse being well collected) by pressing in both heels, leaning back in the saddle, and raising the

bridle-hand, so that the horse will come to a
stop with the hind legs well under the mass. At
the moment the halt is effected the hand should
release the tension upon the reins, and the heels

HALT FROM THE GALLOP.

should be withdrawn from the flanks, and the
horse be permitted to rest.

In the same manner he should bring the
horse to a halt from the trot. He may then
practise the horse in coming to a halt from
the gallop, at first putting the horse into a

slow united pace. As the forehand is about to take the weight in some stride, he should quickly press both heels against the sides of the horse, lean back in the saddle, and raise the bridle-hand. The result of these movements will be that the hind legs will be carried under the mass, and be planted so that they will receive the shock of the sudden halt; and when the fore legs again reach the ground the horse will be stationary. The rider should then lower the bridle-hand and withdraw his heels from the flanks, and the horse will be at rest. By gradual lessons he may teach the horse to come to a halt from higher rates of speed, and even to come to a half-halt or to a finished halt in any stride by the pressure of the heels and the bending back of the body, without making any use of the reins.[1] It was by a combination of this exercise, and of that of the preceding chapter, that I was able to make my horses perform the gallop changes without the use of the reins.

[1] "He went at a gallop straight at the wall, only stopping when the rider brought him up with the spurs just as his nose would have touched the bricks."—Account of the Training of Alidor. London Times, June 1, 1883.

CHAPTER VII.

BACKING.

THE preliminary lessons in backing — that is, those given on foot — may be followed at any time after the horse has been put into the snaffle-bridle; but the horse cannot be taught to back smoothly and lightly under the rider until it has been carried as far in its training as the gallop in the double-reined bridle.

With a little care, the horse may be made to go backward with action as level and regular as in the forward movements, and to make turns and changes of direction with the same precision as if advancing. The first lessons are to be given with the trainer on foot. Standing at the near-side of the horse, he should grasp with his left hand the snaffle-reins at even lengths under the horse's chin, and with his right hand give a whip-tap upon the animal's rump. As soon as an impulse is procured, he should carry his left hand towards the chest of the horse, so that the leg or legs being flexed will take a step to the rear, instead of to the front; this one step having been taken, he will again tap the horse upon the rump, release the tension upon the reins, and let the

BACKING. THE IMPULSE.

horse take a few steps forward without its coming to a full halt. Then he should demand two or more steps to the rear, and require a few steps forward before the horse is allowed to get heavy or come to a halt. These steps to the rear may

be practised until the horse will go any number
of steps backwards, lightly and smoothly; but a
forward movement must always be demanded
before the horse rests. A tap of the whip on
either flank while the horse is backing will make
a change of direction opposite to the side upon
which the whip-tap is delivered. To make the
horse turn to the left in backing, the trainer may
stand on the off-side of the horse and take the
reins in his right hand, the whip in his left, or he
may reach over the back of the horse and apply
the whip to the off-side of the animal. These
lessons in backing should be given from time
to time, with sufficient frequency to insure that
the horse does not forget that which has been
demanded.

After the horse has been confirmed in obedience to the effects of the curb-bit by the
various lessons up to the gallop changes, the
trainer should teach it to back when he is mounted.
He will bring the horse in hand in place, and
give an increased pressure of his legs against the
animal's flanks. The moment an impulse is
secured, he will carry back the forces of the forehand, and decrease the pressure of his heels, so

that the horse will step to the rear with the leg
which is flexed ; and the step having been taken
to the rear, he will close his legs against the
flanks, and decrease the tension upon the reins

BACKING.

so that the horse will move forward. By degrees
the horse will be made to go any distance to the
rear, the rider taking care that the horse is perfectly straight, and that it does not lose its lightness. In backing, the rider must never let the

horse get from under the control of his heels, which should be held close to the side, to regulate the speed, and to enable him to demand the forward movement at any step. To change direction in backing, there will be an increased pressure of the rider's heel on the side opposite to the change, and a slightly increased tension of the rein of the same side; that is, in changing direction in backing to the left, the right heel of the rider and the right rein will give the increased effects.

CHAPTER VIII.

JUMPING.

ALL horses intended for saddle uses should be taught to jump willingly and confidently. The usual practice of chasing a mounted horse over a long bar by the threatening motions of a lashed whip held by an assistant cannot accomplish that which a horseman should desire. A horse "trained" in such a manner is not only very apt to become a "refuser," but it is so hurried and excited that it is impossible that it should jump with precision and safety. I teach my horses to jump over an obstacle so narrow that the temptation to avoid it by going off to one side or the other is offered, and when it once is disciplined to go directly for the obstacle, the idea of refusing a possible jump, or of running out, does not present itself to the animal's mind. One of the gates I use with trained horses is but fourteen inches wide, and this is taken, without an effort to avoid it, by a horse which was the most difficult to discipline of any of the animals

I have handled for the past five years. The horse I employed to illustrate my method for this chapter was a young mare that had never been asked to face an obstacle until it came into my hands, and I was still riding it in the breaker's saddle, as a precaution against plunging, for which I suspected it had a predilection; yet in the second lesson I rode it over a hurdle less than four feet wide, and it made no attempt to avoid the jump.[1]

I do not call upon a young horse to take leaps higher than three feet, as the animal must not be discouraged; but as it becomes stronger and more confident in its powers, the trainer may raise the obstacle to any reasonable height, with a certainty that the horse will make the attempt, and that it will have possession of its wits in avoiding a mistake. One of my horses (Alidor) became so clever in jumping that I frequently rode it over "doubles" without reins, and it never made a mistake, either in or out of the school.

---

[1] This mare was put to jumping much too soon, as it had no mouth, and but little discipline; but I had no horse that was just entering the lessons in the double bridle, so I had either to take an old schooled horse, or one of the green fillies I had selected for illustrating the early lessons.

During the lessons upon the longe, the horse should be exercised near the gates and hurdles so that it may become accustomed to them. When the horse is ready for its lessons in jumping,

LEADING OVER THE BAR.

which may safely be begun at the end of the work in the snaffle-bridle, the trainer should lead it over a bar that is not more than a foot in height; and after the horse will follow over it quietly, the animal should be made to pass the

obstacle in the longeing circles, or at the length of
the reins, while the trainer stands at one end of
the bar. Gradually the bar should be raised until
the horse must give a smart jump to pass it.
From time to time the animal should be encour-
aged and rewarded, and should it attempt to avoid
the bar it should be at once led back, and be made
to understand that there is but one way of proceed-
ing, *and that directly over the obstacle.* It must
not be punished, but a light tap of the whip may
be given to stimulate the impulses, and the jumps
should be cleanly and quietly made. Colored
rugs, bushes, and other objects which would
usually frighten a horse if it were made to face
them without some preparation, should be placed
against the bar until the horse will jump anything the trainer's mind can devise (I used to
longe Alidor over a pony), the man being careful
not to require too much effort on the part of the
horse, and not to fatigue or dishearten it.

The horse should now be ridden over the
obstacles, first as in the lessons in hand, being
walked over the low bar, and then being trot-
ted up to the bar raised to a height of twenty-
four to thirty inches, so that it must give a true

jump to get over. The snaffle-bit only should be used in these early lessons, and the tension upon the reins only sufficient to guide the horse to the obstacle. The man should make no effort to

JUMPING IN HAND.

raise the horse, or to indicate where it is to take off for the jump; and in landing, the animal should receive a very slight support from the hand. Any rough treatment, particularly any severe use of the bit, will be disastrous. The horse should look upon the leaping lessons with pleasure, and it should be rewarded for every well-made jump.

When the horse jumps fairly well from the trot, it should be brought to the obstacle in the walk; then it should be taught to jump perfectly from the halt. The horse should not be ridden over obstacles in the gallop until it has been taught to gallop well in the double-reined bridle.

As the horse approaches the obstacle in the walk, the trot, or the gallop, it should be gently united, so that it may exert all that are necessary of its powers; and upon alighting, it should again be collected to proceed in exactly the same pace and speed with which it approached the obstacle. The higher the obstacle the slower should be the pace, the more closely united should be the forces, and the more vigorous should be the action. In a broad jump the speed should be rapid enough to give momentum, but it should not be so fast that the horse cannot collect itself for the exertion. The most difficult thing in jumping is to determine exactly how much assistance the hand should afford as the horse alights; the tension upon the reins should never be so great as to impede the horse in its efforts to land safely, and yet if the horse seeks some support it must find it. Should the horse ever refuse a leap, or get into the habit of jumping carelessly, it should be

THE FIRST LEAP OF A YOUNG HORSE.

put back to the early lessons. But it will be the fault of the rider if a horse once properly trained ever becomes disorderly in leaping.

Only riders with the firmest of seats and the lightest of hands should use the curb-bit in jumping. In case of a fall in jumping the rider should keep his hold upon the reins, at least until he is assured that he is free of the stirrups. It is better to run the risk of being stepped upon by the horse than to be dragged by the stirrup, and the rider should never part from his horse if it can be avoided.

CHAPTER IX.

VICES, TRICKS, AND FAULTS.

I HAVE been training horses for many years, and I have failed to observe in them any traits of character which might be designated as noble, or which showed anything above a very low order of intelligence. The horse is so nervous and apprehensive that it never completely gives its confidence to man, and it exhibits more of the reasoning powers in its defences and resistances than in the direction of obedience. Fortunately the horse is a creature of one idea, and until we can obtain control over it by discipline, it is possible to thwart its malevolent intentions by a counter-attack. I am far from saying that all horses are naturally vicious; but I do say that the horse does not voluntarily obey the demands of its master, and that he who depends upon its willing obedience is in a precarious position, unless it be from a heartless drudge that has lost all visions of freedom. Restraint and control must be irksome to all animals, and it is natural that the high-spirited horse should attempt to escape restraint and control. It is in the injudicious endeavors to combat these efforts of the horse to avoid the tyranny of man that the vices, tricks, and faults of the animal have their origin. If in its early mutiny the horse is foiled, it will soon forbear; but one success will be remembered through scores of defeats. When discipline has become a second nature to the horse, the man can depend upon its obedience, until by accident or carelessness the animal is shown by what a slender chain it has been enslaved. It is far more difficult to restore discipline with these spoiled horses than to establish it from the first in the unbroken colt; but it is not impossible.

It is when it is in that state of nervous irritability known as "freshness," from want of work, that most of the disorderly conduct of the horse has its beginning. A horse that is "fresh" should be treated with great care; and if it gives a few plunges when first mounted, or is shy of objects with which it should be perfectly familiar, the rider should not punish it, but should rather take little notice of its misconduct, and push it forward in a brisk trot until it becomes more composed. He may turn its head away from that about which it shows fear, and in this manner he can make it pass anything. A shy horse should never be made *to face* the object that affrights it, until it has lost its fear.

Should the animal begin to misconduct itself while the man is mounting, he should have it led forward and vault into the saddle while the horse is in motion, or have a leg up from the attendant who leads it. When the horse is calmed by exercise, he should bring it to a halt, and mount and dismount until he assures himself that the horse will stand quietly for such purposes. Should the horse have the habit of being restless while being mounted, the man should make it extend itself by placing the fore feet far in advance of their normal position when the animal is at rest, and by then handling the horse, pulling upon the stirrup-leathers, and bearing his weight upon his arms placed on the saddle. Then, letting the horse take its natural position, he should quietly mount in the usual way, and walk the animal off.

Should the horse turn its croup to one hand or to the other, and leave the line of progress, its head should be pulled over to the side towards which the croup is bent; this will straighten the horse, and the desired direction may then be taken.

Should the horse stop and wheel to the rear, the rider should at once make it complete the wheel, while its opposition is to the other hand; and when the animal is straight in the original direction, he should push it forward in any pace that it will take, gaining a composed and regular pace when he can.

Should the animal come to a halt, lower its head, gather its legs under the body, and arch its back, the rider should not attempt to force it to move, for it will certainly bolt, and perhaps " buck." By quietly moving either the forehand or the croup to one side or to the other, he can induce the horse to let down the back and raise the head, when he will be able to move the horse slowly forward.

Should the horse stand stiffly, with its legs apart and its head extended upwards, and refuse to move, the rider should not attempt to force it forward. By waiting until he can bend the head to the right or to the left, he can reduce the rigidity of the animal, and then be able to move it forward.

As I have said, a shy horse should have its head turned away from the object which frightens it, and be made to pass along in a movement resembling that upon two paths. The nearer it is brought to the object which causes its terror the better; for if it be once brought quite close to that which has seemed dangerous, it will be taught that its fears were groundless.

A horse which rears viciously can be cured by a course of suppling. I have had for four years a horse whose defence took this form, and it had several times thrown itself backwards with its former owner; but, although I have ridden it in the high-school movements, in jumping and in *le jeu de barre*, it has never offered, since it was put through a course of suppling, to rise higher than I have demanded.

9

When a horse rears, the rider should close his heels against its sides, and, as the forehand comes down, take a bearing upon the snaffle-reins, then push the animal forward, not violently, — for that would induce plunging, — but firmly and quietly. If, when the horse rears, the rider feels from the sinking of the croup that the animal is about to fall over, he should take his feet out of the stirrups, grasp the mane, and throw himself away from the horse. A rearing horse always gets behind the hand before it rises, and this fact indicates a prevention. But if the jaw is so suppled that it yields to every touch of the bit, the animal cannot rear; for the head would drop and the mouth would open at a light tension upon the reins.

If a "bolter" has intelligence enough to receive discipline, the vice may be cured by teaching the animal to come to a halt at the application of the spurs. Alidor bolted in his early lessons; but after he had been schooled. he never attempted to escape control. If a horse bolts through nervousness, there is no cure of which I have any knowledge, and I know of no bit which will check the animal.

It is difficult to break a *plunging horse* of its vice, because it is hard to get control over the animal while it is plunging. When a horse plunges it should have its head held up, and it should be pushed forward until it takes some regular pace. If it plunges from high spirits only, it will probably drop the trick when it has been carefully ridden; but if plunging become an established vice, it cannot be guarded against. As an experiment, I took a horse with this vice confirmed, and taught it to plunge as a movement, thinking that the animal would not voluntarily perform that which had become a labor. I was mistaken; the horse continued to plunge when it was fresh, and I could never depend upon its steadiness. This horse had the "buck's eye," of which I have spoken, and was usually very foolish.

When a horse refuses to leave its company, or to go in a certain direction, or is otherwise *restive*, it should be turned about several times by drawing the rein which finds the least resistance, and by pressing in the heel of the same side. This "rolling-up" of the animal confuses it, and makes it forget its intention, and the rider may then direct it where he pleases. It is the custom in most European cavalry regiments for every man, in troop or in squadron drill, to ride his horse out singly from the ranks, and to return slowly to his place. In many cases this could not be accomplished without this "rolling-up," as the horses are usually loath to leave their companions. I know some regiments where this movement is not employed, and in which there are not ten horses in a hundred which will singly leave the barrack-yard, even with the riding-master's whip behind them.

If the horse tries to rub the leg of the rider against a wall or other obstacle, the head of the animal should be pulled into the obstacle, when the design of the animal will be frustrated.

I have no advice to give to the rider who finds his horse "running away," beyond that of sticking to the animal, and of taking intermittent pulls upon its mouth until he finds the pace decreasing, when he may be able to bring it to halt, or to a desired rate of speed.

THE END.

www.ingramcontent.com/pod-product-compliance
Lightning Source LLC
Chambersburg PA
CBHW030613270326
41927CB00007B/1153